Eight Ate

A Feast of Homonym Riddles

by Marvin Terban
illustrated by Giulio Maestro

CLARION BOOKS
NEW YORK

Clarion Books
a HarperCollins Publishers LLC imprint
195 Broadway, New York, NY 10007
Text copyright © 1982 by Marvin Terban
Illustration copyright © 1982 by Giulio Maestro
First Clarion paperback edition, 1982; reissued, 2007.

www.clarionbooks.com

Printed in China

Library of Congress Cataloging-in-Publication Data

Terban, Marvin.
Eight ate.
Summary: A collection of original riddles, each using a
homonym as the answer : bizarre-bazaar, foul-fowl,
and similar pairs of words.
1. Riddles—Juvenile literature. 2 English language—
Homonyms—Juvenile Literature. [1. Riddles. 2. English
language—Homonyms] I. Maestro, Giulio, ill. II. Title.
PN6371.5.T43 1982 818' 5402   81-12203
ISBN: 0-89919-067-7
ISBN: 0-89919-086-3 (pa)

ISBN-13: 978-0-618-76676-5 ISBN-10: 0-618-76676-6

LEO 20 19 18 17 16 15 14 13 12

For David and Jennifer
who never look alike
but sometimes sound alike

What do you say in the evening
to a soldier in shining armor?

"Night-night, Knight!"

How does Moose begin a letter
to his cousin?

"Dear Deer..."

What would we do if we found bad plants
spoiling our lawn?

We'd weed.

How do you say, "Run away, small jumping insect that lives on a dog!"?

"Flee, flea!"

What is an animal with a rough-sounding
voice that cowboys ride?

A hoarse horse.

What is a complete opening in the ground?

A whole hole.

What marks are left by the messy fingers
of the king's son?

Prince prints.

What did the fancy flying machine
call the undecorated one?

A plain plane.

What is a smelly chicken?

A foul fowl.

What do you call a less expensive bird?

A cheaper cheeper.

What did the teacher say when trying to match kids to parents?

"Who's whose?"

Who is married to Uncle Beetle?

Aunt Ant.

What is a small group of musicians that
isn't allowed to play?

A banned band.

What does a broken window feel?

A pain in the pane.

What do you call a bucket that
has seen a ghost?

A pale pail.

How did the plate introduce the potatoes
to the steak?

"Meet meat!"

What on your face is first aware
of a good smell?

The nose knows.

What is a large animal with thick fur
but no clothes on?

A bare bear.

What is perfume that is mailed?

Sent scent.

What did the math student shout when
he added up all the numbers?

169,438,299,001
477,893,429,999
238,694,445,666
598,432,698,790
+ 664,211,115,039
─────────────────
2,148,669,988,495

"Some sum!"

What is the loud, sad crying of the biggest
animal in the ocean?

A whale wail.

What is a weird street of shops
that sell incredible things?

A bizarre bazaar.

Two ran the race, but only…

One won.

What is a reddish-purple vegetable
that is all worn out?

A beat beet.

What will a foot doctor do for you?

He'll heal your heel.

If they are not here,
where are they?

They're there!

What do you call the totally uninterested
directors of a company?

A bored board.

What did the male sheep call
to the female sheep?

"Yoo hoo, you ewe!"

What is rabbit fur?

Hare hair.

When two couples go to a restaurant together,
they ask for a table...

For four.

What are nervous little outdoor
cloth houses?

Tense tents.

What are groups of sailors on
an ocean pleasure trip?

Cruise crews.

What do you use to make blossom bread
and petal pie?

Flower flour.

Why didn't the cloud of very fine drops
wet us?

The mist missed.

What did the teacher say to Orville when
his letters slanted too much to the left?

"Write right, Wright!"

How does the short man greet
the tall man?

"Hi, high."

If you don't listen over there,
where should you listen?

Hear here!

What does the man who looks at oceans do all day?

Sees seas.

What did the rich man give his rabbit?

A 14-carat carrot.

If a big rock is brave, what do you call
one that's even braver?

A bolder boulder.

What did the king say when he wanted
someone to ask him for favors?

"Pleas, please!"

What do you call a hot drink
on the golf course?

Tee tea.

After the third grade marched forward,
what did the principal say?

"Bring the fourth forth!"

What coins can detect odors?

Cents sense scents.

What is clam strength?

Mussel muscle.

What is a tale about a tenant?

A roomer rumor.

If a devil is completely sinful,
what is an angel?

Wholly holy.

Why did Miss Muffet put her bowl
on the scale?

It was a way to weigh her whey.

What is a string of jewels
for someone with no neck?

A neckless necklace.

What do you call the sharp, curved nails
on a crab who is playing Santa?

Claus claws.

If two apples are a couple of apples,
what are two pears?

A pear pair.

What is a great accomplishment using
the ends of your legs?

A feet feat.

What does a female deer use for baking?

Doe dough.

What is a sailor's bellybutton?

A naval navel.

How do you say: "Make that wool
into a sweater, little insect!"

"Knit, nit!"

What did the wizard ask himself when he couldn't decide whom to marry?

"Which witch?"

What is a good-looking,
horse-drawn carriage?

A handsome hansom.

What is a pier for doctors only?

A Doc dock.

If the stars swirled and the comets curled,
what did the Earth do?

The world whirled.

If four couples went to a restaurant, how many people dined?

Eight ate.

About the Author

Marvin Terban teaches English and history at The Columbia Grammar and Preparatory School in New York City. This book, his first, began as a teaching game in one of his English classes.

Mr. Terban was born in Chelsea, Massachusetts, graduated from Tufts University, and earned a master's degree in media at Columbia University. He, his wife Karen, and their two children live in New York City.

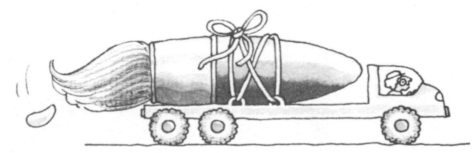

About the Artist

Giulio Maestro is a freelance illustrator of children's books, who has written and illustrated several books of his own. He graduated from Cooper Union Art School in New York City and studied at Pratt Graphics Center.

Mr. Maestro was assistant art director and designer for a creative advertising studio in New York before turning full-time to illustration. He and his wife Betsy, a children's book writer, live with their two children in Madison, Connecticut.